W9-AYC-477

THE SHADOW
OF THE CROSS

THE SHADOW
OF THE CROSS
Studies in Self-Denial

WALTER J. CHANTRY
*{Retired Pastor of Grace Baptist Church,
Carlisle, Pennsylvania}*

THE BANNER OF TRUTH TRUST

THE BANNER OF TRUTH TRUST
3 Murrayfield Road, Edinburgh EH12 6EL, UK
P.O. Box 621, Carlisle, PA 17013, USA

*

© Walter J. Chantry 1981
First published 1981
Reprinted 1989
Reprinted 2001
Reprinted 2005
Reprinted 2009

ISBN-13: 978 0 85151 331 7

*

Printed in the USA by
Versa Press, Inc.
East Peoria, IL

Contents

1

UNTO HIM WHO DIED
AND ROSE

For whether we be beside ourselves, it is to God: or whether we be sober, it is for your cause. For the love of Christ constraineth us; because we thus judge, that if one died for all, then were all dead: and that he died for all, that they which live should not henceforth live unto themselves, but unto him which died for them, and rose again. [2 Corinthians 5:13-15]

Self-denial is a practice which lies very near to the heart of true religion. Without its exercise there can be no conversion to Christ. Qualities most basic to a Christian frame of heart — notably humility and meekness — would dissolve without its active expression. Self-denial awaits the sons of God as they enter upon their private devotions. It stands at the threshold of witnessing and other service to our holy Lord. It is a most painful element in each struggle after holiness. Denial of self is the key to the solution of numerous practical questions which perplex the sober-minded believer of today. A right understanding of this basic biblical demand would silence a host of errors regarding evangelism, sanctification, and practical living.

Yet too little is written and preached upon self-denial. Sometimes the most profound truths are ignored because they are obvious. Perhaps this particular biblical truth lies forgotten because of the perversions of it in the past. There have been such varied forms of fanatic asceticism in the history of the church, that some might shy away from the subject. A recent generation of preachers offered self-denial as a step to a 'second work of grace'. Perhaps there remain from the same source intricate and confusing dissections of human personality which becloud the simple term 'self'. One does not wish to be identified with these elements. All of this has contributed to silence on a vital theme of Scripture.

Of all people, however, Reformed Christians should resurrect the biblical teaching on self-denial from its unjust obscurity. It is not the property of Medieval Flagellants. We dare not yield it as the property of the 'deeper life' movement. It was the Son of God who said, 'Whosoever will come after me, let him deny himself, and take up his cross, and follow me' [Mark 8:34].

True Calvinism always leads to the appreciation of self-denial. When the doctrines of grace are warmly and experimentally preached, denial of self is necessarily one of the chief experiences of the soul. Each one of the doctrines infinitely exalts the most high God and humbles the sinful and human self as a mere worm. What is it that you love about the doctrines of God's sovereignty and of human depravity? Is it not the wonder and realization of it all flooding your soul? Is it not the blessed slaying of self-admiration, self-indulgence, self-satisfaction, self-determination . . . all of self? Is it not the rising beam of love to God with the prayer of Psalm 115:1, 'Not unto us, O Lord, not unto us, but unto thy name give glory, for thy mercy, and for thy truth's sake'? Indeed it is the wrenching of our hearts from serving trite personal interests to glorifying God and enjoying him for ever.

Nothing leads to self-repudiation so much as spiritual meditation on the corruption and wickedness of your heart. If your soul has grasped human depravity you have been forced to deny yourself. When Ezekiel delivered God's promise of putting his Spirit within men, one of the results of this gift of the Spirit was expressed in Ezekiel 36:31: 'Then shall ye remember your own evil ways, and your doings that were not good, and shall loathe *yourselves* in your own sight for your iniquities and for your abominations.' No man can conclude in his heart, '*in me* dwelleth no good thing' [Romans 7:18] and then continue to live for himself. One great benefit of the biblical truths called Calvinism is that they humble men in the dust. They make a man feel that 'the whole head is sick, and the whole heart faint. From the sole of the foot even unto the head there is no soundness in it; but wounds, and bruises, and putrifying sores' [Isaiah 1:5–6]. When this truth has seeped into the innermost man, he can no longer live for himself, but cries with Job, 'Wherefore I abhor *myself*, and repent in dust and ashes' [Job 42:6]. Calvinism that does not humble has missed its mark.

But there is a positive side as well. While man's self-esteem is crushed, his esteem for the Lord God of hosts is established. God's glory and grace strike and captivate the heart. The absolute freeness of his mercy in Jesus Christ prompts the soul to join the heavenly host which falls down before him day and night singing 'Alleluia; glory, and honour, and power unto the Lord our God'. With a vision of his sovereign and infinite mercy, a new sense of frustration and heartache fills the soul. It is not the old cry of the selfish heart hungry to satisfy its own appetites. It is the longing to hallow his Name. Oh, to render honour to the Saviour! 'What wilt thou have me to do, Lord?' Is there not something I can do for thee? Implicit in the prayers of a soul enraptured by the glories of the King is the denial of self.

The doctrines of grace are not merely a philosophy which gives the best and most logical answers to the profound questions of life. They are that. But more, they stir the inner man to self-abnegation and love for Jehovah. This act of worship before the throne of the Almighty opens a fountain of devotion which must then flow out at every level of decision and action in the practical life. Self-denial is a vital link between doctrine and devotion on the one hand and between devotion and practice on the other. The truth that I am a foul rebel and that God is the author of amazing grace leads to the devotional act of self-denial, which in turn must demonstrate itself in daily living. The true test of your Calvinism comes just here. How low is self and how high is God in your heart? Almost every moment of your life offers a test. The logical conclusion, the practical application of every element of God's sovereign grace, is found in the expression of 2 Corinthians 5:15, 'He died for all, that they which live should not henceforth live unto themselves, but unto him which died for them and rose again.' This was Paul's grand explanation of the Christian life.

Paul's word 'henceforth' in verse 15 implies something about the past. 'Should not *henceforth* live unto themselves' is an indirect testimony to his past life. It is an accurate description of all men as born in Adam — they 'live unto themselves'. Selfishness is the controlling force of sinful living. It is this motive which pulsates through the natural mind, emotions and will — self-pleasing, self-serving, living for self.

Often the Bible describes sin as selfishness. Isaiah 53:6: 'All we like sheep have gone astray; we have turned every one to *his own way*'. The ways are as varied as the personalities and tastes of the sheep. But each one is 'his own way.' 2 Timothy 3:1–2 states the obvious in shocking terms: 'This know also that in the last days perilous times shall come. For men shall be *lovers of their own selves* . . .' That is the disgusting reality of our generation. Men are making decisions with only one consideration, 'their own selves'. Everyone is shouting for his own rights. Brazen men and women boast of their shame. They do their own thing. It has become the vocal philosophy defended in our day. There is no concern about neighbour, or children for that matter. The chief object of modern men's love is 'their own selves'.

Peter, describing those who walk in the flesh, said, 'Presumptuous are they, *self-willed*' [2 Peter 2:10]. The sinful mind is devoted to private opinions. Nothing infuriates like the suggestion to a sinner that he is mistaken. Ahab gathered 400 men to tell him what he wished to hear, but was still indignant when the lonely voice of Micaiah contradicted his private views. The sinful emotions are stirred most deeply by self-love. Wills are devoted to self-interest.

The roots of this depravity are quite evident in very young children. Babies may not show all the ugly outworkings of sin, but their selfishness is quite apparent. Any time of the day or night they will howl when their little egos are annoyed. Brothers and sisters have noticed how small children are self-seeking. When treats are being given, a 'me first' attitude prevails. Small children want the chief attention. It is all self-serving. This all-demanding self-will matures into that of a grasping adult. Though clever devices will make the selfishness polite and genteel, all of life outside of Christ is for one thing – self!

Our Saviour's parables are filled with sinners' self-worship. The prodigal son said, 'Give me the portion of goods that falleth *to me*' [Luke 15:12]. Like him, we have wanted to spend health, time, talent, riches on selfish gratification, selfish ambitions, selfish pleasures, selfish pride. Self is the idol to which all men naturally bow. There is the example of the rich fool in Luke 12 who kept using the personal pronoun 'I' in all his plans. Our Lord said, 'So is he that layeth up treasure *for himself*, and is not rich *toward* God.'

Paul, by his 'henceforth', admits 'I was like that too. I built a reputation as a zealot for orthodoxy. I laboured for my own righteousness. I lived for Paul.' But that is past now. Verse 17: 'If any man be in Christ, he is a new creature: old things are passed away; behold, all things are become new.' Becoming a Christian involves a complete re-ordering of priorities. Once self was first and God second, or third, after other men. But now my thoughts bow to his Word above my private opinions. My feelings and desires take second place to his will. I love him and choose to please him rather than myself.

This little man Paul understood that denial of self is demanded at the start of following Christ. The specific ultimatum is aimed at a different item for each person. Covetous men must deny themselves as in the case of the rich young ruler — selling all and giving to the poor. For proud Paul, weaving his self-righteousness, it was necessary to call his righteousness dung that he might win Christ. But all of this is implicit.

2 Corinthians 5:15 is much more explicit. It is describing the ongoing goal of the Christian life, 'that they which live should not *henceforth* live unto themselves, but unto him which died for them, and rose again.' This is the continual attitude that marks every soul truly born of God. Here is Paul's longing heart, 'that I may know him' and 'be found in him'. The great desire is to live for the Saviour at any cost to himself.

'Henceforth' is prospective. It is for evermore! 1 Peter 4:2, 'He no longer should live the rest of his time in the flesh to the lusts of men, but *to the will of God.*' The rest of his days on earth will be unto God. The glorious ease of eternity will follow, when there will be no competition from a twisted self and all of his being will yield praise unto him that loved us and washed us from our sins in his own blood.

Such a high objective, described negatively as 'no longer living for self,' and positively as living for Christ, arose from Paul's meditations on the cross of

Christ. The apostle's mind turned to the question, 'Why did Jesus Christ die?' There are many sides to answering such an important question. But under the influence of the Spirit, the apostle teaches that our Lord's death was not designed to provide selfish men with eternal life while they remained abandoned to self-serving. A vital part of Christ's intention was to redirect the motivation of all whom his blood-shedding would make alive. As he struggled up Calvary's hill and bled upon it, his aim was to eradicate self-love and implant the love of God in the hearts of men. One can only increase as the other decreases.

Denial of self is not a spiritual form of masochism. Pain inflicted upon self is not intended to be the goal of any spiritual exercise. Here the flagellants were mistaken in assuming that suffering and unpleasantness would in itself yield improvement to men. Self-denial is only wholesome when attended with an equal measure of living unto him who died and rose again. Self-denial is the birth pang of spiritual joy. No woman seeks birth pangs, but she willingly endures them for the pleasure of cradling an infant in her arms. It is because of the sheer delight of living for the glory of Jehovah and the satisfaction of dwelling in the presence of his majestic fellowship that Christians submit to the agonies of self-denial. It is never an end in itself.

Fasting is never beneficial alone. But fasting as a means to humbling one's soul before the throne of God is of enormous benefit. Then all of the energies and attention devoted to eating and digestion may be gathered up and redirected to earnest prayer. At every level self-denial is only beneficial when the mental exercise — streams of affection and energies of the will which once served self — is redirected unto him who died and rose again. Otherwise the heart will be like the house our Saviour described as cleansed from one devil [Luke 11:24–26]. If one devil of self-interest is swept from the soul, seven self-schemes worse than the first will return with it unless the soul is fully employed with living unto him who died and rose again.

Unfortunately, too few Christians keep this great objective sufficiently before them as life in Christ proceeds. In commending Timothy to the church at Philippi Paul remarked, 'For I have no man like-minded, who will naturally care for your state. *For all seek their own, not the things which are Jesus Christ's'* [Philippians 2:20–21]. Even among clergymen the remaining blight is 'seeking their own.' The need of the hour is that they seek 'the things which are Jesus Christ's'. Few such pastors may be found. Earlier in the same chapter Paul had urged the congregation, 'Look not every man *on his own things*, but every man also on the things of others.' This repeated emphasis in Scripture marks the centre-point of battle in the Christian life. To fight a good fight of faith a banner must be raised on which is printed, 'Henceforth not unto ourselves but unto him who died and rose again.'

Every step of progress in sanctification brings the Christian back to the dreadful battleground where many a tear has been shed and many a drop of blood spilled. If you are in Christ it is a familiar scene. There before you is the grisly old enemy to spiritual progress standing astride the path of obedience to Christ – SELF! This monster cries out daily to be served. He challenges the dominion of Jesus Christ and opposes every devotion of time, energy and love to the Lord. But it is a strange war that we may win only by feeling ourselves the painful blows we give. Every denial of self is felt keenly. How we would love to change the scene of combat! But on every occasion when we are serious about advancing in righteousness, we must contend with self.

In the Sermon on the Mount our Lord taught, 'And if thy right eye offend thee, pluck it out, and cast it from thee: for it is profitable for thee that one of thy members should perish, and not that thy whole body should be cast into hell. And if thy right hand offend thee, cut it off, and cast it from thee: for it is profitable for thee that one of thy members should perish, and not that thy whole body should be cast into hell' [Matthew 5:29–30]. Such vivid language, of course, does not suggest doing physical harm to oneself. Yet it does teach that dismemberment of self is essential to triumph over recurring falls into temptation. If only there were a sugary alternative! But plucking out an eye or amputating a limb, with the consequent shock to one's entire system, is still the prescribed remedy of the Great Physician.

Often when plain directives of Christ's Word have shown us the way to the higher ground of serving Christ, we have hesitated in horror. We have cast about for another way. But there is none other – deny self, live unto him who died and rose again.

Many longings for revival are a bit unrealistic.

What is your notion of revival? You would like to see multitudes pressing into the kingdom, would you not? You long for worship experiences in which your heart expands with wonder, love and praise. You wish to see Christ's church mighty, conquering her foes, driving all enemies of truth and righteousness before her triumphant march through our age. But how do you envision yourself in the midst of such blessing? There you sit in the church and it all happens by the mighty power of God! And you are there to drink in the joy.

But are pastors prepared to double their efforts as multitudes of babes cry for milk from the Word? Are elders willing to pare off their schedules all personal relaxation and ease in order to devote themselves to the multiplied tasks involved in keeping up with God's doings in revival times? Are all believers prepared for the overwhelming demands on time and energy when God's presence is felt in the midst of his people? Then there will be no time for casual T.V. programmes, vacation trips, or relaxing evenings. There is a cost to the saints in revival. Life-styles will be altered.

It is to be feared that many in the church desire all their toys for self and revival too. While many moan that God has not rent the heavens and come down, very few deny themselves of food to fast. Self is not denied whole days while saints keep not silence till he make Jerusalem a praise in the earth! No axe is being laid to the root of self. Is it not time for those who are in earnest about revival to declare a relentless war on self, resolving afresh that henceforth they will not live unto themselves but unto him who died and rose again? Not a once-for-all encounter, but a life devoted to denying self and living every hour unto him who died and rose again. All the great spiritual delights we long for come into the world of a Christian's experience attended with birth-pangs of self-denial.

2

TAKE UP YOUR CROSS

And he said to them all, If any man will come after me, let him deny himself, and take up his cross daily, and follow me. For whosoever will save his life shall lose it: but whosoever will lose his life for my sake, the same shall save it. [Luke 9:23, 24]

Only one entrance may be found to the Kingdom of God. There is a narrow gate set at the head of the path of life. 'Strait is the gate, and narrow is the way, which leadeth unto life, and few there be that find it' [Matthew 7:14]. No one with an inflated ego can squeeze through the door. There must be self-effacement, self-repudiation, self-denial even to become a disciple [a student] of Jesus Christ.

Our Saviour made his demand quite clear by explicitly requiring self-denial. He then re-emphasized the point by using a vivid illustration of renouncing one's self — an illustration he would soon seal with his blood, 'Let him deny himself, and take up his cross'. Six times in the Gospels our great Prophet refers to his followers' taking up a cross. It was one of his favourite illustrations of self-denial. At other times he would speak of selling all, or of losing one's life.

'Cross' is a word that first brings to our minds the picture of our Lord on Calvary. We think of him bleeding while fastened to an instrument designed to inflict an agonizing death. Then perhaps we expand the idea of taking up a cross by thinking of Stephen who was stoned to death, or of Peter and

John, who were beaten and put into prison, and of other martyrs across the ages. In the light of such courageous physical suffering, the Christian at ease may say to himself, 'I don't have any cross to bear'. Perhaps this repeated demand of Christ even brings alarm to your consciences as you read it over and over in Scripture.

Some who call themselves 'Christian' in fact have never taken up their crosses. Being ignorant of the experience of self-execution, of self-denial, they are of necessity strangers to Christ. Our Lord himself intended his illustration and his demand to deepen alarm in such individuals. If this is your condition, then there can be no relief to conviction but in taking up your cross and following him.

Others, however, are true servants of Christ but feel a sense of dismay through a misunderstanding of our Lord's demand. It is quite possible to have taken up your cross and not to know it. Careful examination of our Lord's meaning will then be an encouragement.

In either case, the subject is vital to you. Your Master's life was dominated by a cross. He has called you also to a life with a cross. This clear gospel note is so easy to forget in flabby Western society. With a great chorus of custom, advertisement and temptation this world is beckoning you to a life of self-indulgence. Your flesh is drawn to that appeal, and will fall in with the world's suggestions. But the Lord of glory has called you to a life of self-denial, to a cross.

The demand of bearing a cross is *universal*. It is made of all who follow Christ, without exception.

Our Lord addressed these words 'to all', not to a select few who walked nearer to Christ. Mark 8:34 indicates that this mandate was not issued to the twelve alone. It was spoken 'when he had called the people unto him with his disciples'. The cross is required for 'any man' who will go after him. There are no peculiar cases released from this necessity.

Repeatedly our Lord was emphatic that none could be considered his disciple in any sense unless he bore a cross. 'And he that taketh not his cross, and followeth after me, is not worthy of me' [Matthew 10:38]. Again in Luke 14:27 our Saviour turned to a multitude following him, to insist, 'Whosoever doth not bear his cross, and come after me, cannot be my disciple'. It is an absolute impossibility to be a Christian without self-denial. Whether you live in a Christian land or in a culture hostile to God's Word, you must bear a cross. The only way to avoid the cross is to follow the world to hell. As verse 24 explains, 'For whosoever will save his life shall lose it'. The 'for' indicates a connection with the preceding verse. Religion without self-denial will not endure the judgment.

It is this most obvious aspect of our Lord's teaching which has been forgotten or ignored by modern evangelism. Anxious to bring sinners to life, peace and joy in the Lord, evangelists have failed even to mention that Christ insists upon denial of self at the outset. Having failed to pass on our Lord's requirement, and forgetting it themselves, evangelists have never questioned whether their 'converts' with self-centred lives are true followers of Christ. Assuming that it is possible for a man to be self-indulgent and

yet heaven-bound, Bible teachers look for some way
to bring ego-centric men to a higher spiritual plane.
Then self-denial is taught as the requirement for a
second work of grace. But our text will show that
unless a man lives a life of self-denial, he has not
received a first work of grace.

Those who save texts demanding a cross for 'the
deeper life' have cheated their hearers in evangelism.
Without a cross there is no following Christ! And
without following Christ there is no life at all! An
impression has been given that many enter life
through a wide gate of believing on Jesus. Then a
few go through the narrow gate of the cross for
deeper spiritual service. On the contrary, the broad
way without self-denial leads to destruction. All who
are saved have entered the fraternity of the cross.

Christ's summons to a cross is *perpetual*. Self-denial
is not an initiation-fee, once paid and for ever
forgotten. Old Christians as well as new converts
must bear a cross. One's cross is not a disposable
item of Christian experience but a life-long burden
in this world.

This conversation apparently took place after
Caesarea Philippi. It was near the end of our Lord's
earthly ministry. Almost three years earlier, Jesus
had called the disciples. We read a partial account
of the call in Luke 5. When they began to follow the
Messiah, there was a painful price of a cross to be
weighed. For Peter it was leaving a beloved father
and abandoning a good fishing business in a quiet
village. For Matthew it was turning his back on the
lucrative tax bureau he directed. Throughout more
than two years there was the painful experience of

poverty, tumult and disgrace in following the Master. Now, as they near the completion of their training, our Lord holds before them the expectation of a cross. Whether you have walked with Christ one year or forty, you must deny yourself still.

You will notice that the text uses the word 'daily'. For a true believer the cross is ubiquitous, lifelong, a daily weight. There is but one depository of the cross, that is the cemetery. We shall not carry the pain of self-denial into the celestial city. But our Lord holds out no hope that the cross will cease to afflict us in this life. It is 'daily', for 'any man'. You must ask yourself, 'Am I bearing a cross today?'

As has been suggested, the cross is *painful*. The term 'cross' has lost all significance if the element of dreadful suffering is taken away. Our Lord endured the most cruel pangs ever inflicted upon a man. But we must recognize that the cross represented *inward* as well as outward pains. To our perfect Lord the inward torture of the cross was far greater than the outward.

Hebrews 12:2 teaches us that Jesus 'endured the cross, despising the shame'. The shame was much more painful to his noble dignity than were the nails and the bleeding to his body. Some have failed to estimate what the cross was to him: the confusion of being made sin before the Father, the embarrassment before his enemies of open judgment by a righteous God. The shame of nakedly identifying with filthy transgressions before men, angels and God, cut his sensitive soul to the quick.

Inward suffering must be the focus of our Lord's teaching in this passage. Our cross is not merely physical suffering. Stephen was not stoned 'daily', yet the Saviour said we must bear a 'daily cross. Even in the worst of times apostles were not imprisoned 'daily'. There is a cross to bear on the best of days as well as on the worst. Peter carried a cross during civil peace as well as in times of strife. A failure to comprehend that inward pain is the worst part of the cross has led some believers to misunderstand our Lord's demand of a daily cross. It is this misunderstanding which may lead to unnecessary alarm and dismay when true saints read our Lord's demand. You may bear a cross unseen by all but your heavenly Father. How often a pastor is surprised to learn of the cross borne by members of the congregation, through trials never imagined by him. The deepest pains of the cross are not publicly visible.

Furthermore, taking up your cross is an *intentional* act. In every passage which records our Lord's mention of a cross for his disciples, he commands them to 'take it up'. The Lord does not force a cross upon any man against his will. He does not strap the cross to a man's back. There are great afflictions for God's people which are imposed by providence. Irresistible sufferings may be the hand of chastisement or of refining mercy. These are trials but not crosses. A cross must be taken up by the one whose self is to be denied painfully.

It was a voluntary submission on Christ's part which brought him to Calvary. 'No man taketh my life from me, but I lay it down of myself' [John 10:18]. Armed soldiers could not seize him. The Son of God delivered himself into their custody. Just so is the daily cross of his disciples. It is the conscious choice of a painful alternative motivated by love for Christ. It may be preceded by an inward struggle similar to that which our Lord knew in Gethsemane. But it is a voluntary choice.

Lastly, the taking up of a cross is *mortal*. It is deadly. Death on the cross may be very slow, but a cross has one objective – it ruthlessly intends to bring death to self. Two parallel ideas in verses 23 and 24 show us that our Lord has this in mind. 'Let him deny himself'. Put to death self-importance, self-satisfaction, self-absorption, self-advancement, self-dependence. And 'whosoever *will lose his life* for my sake'. That's it! Death to self-interest because you serve Christ's honour! Even capitulation of those things which men call legitimate interests, for God's glory!

It is now apparent that Jesus' figure of bearing a cross is an elaboration of his demand for self-denial. *Bearing a cross is every Christian's daily, conscious selection of those options which will please Christ, pain self, and aim at putting self to death.* It is a teaching for the recruit, not merely for the seasoned warrior. It is a requirement for entering the army of God, not merely a call to an élite corps of super-saints with a deeper life. Yet it does hold the clue as well to deepening maturity in Christ. At each stage of growth, more self-denial is required, more painful blows to self, more reckless decision to serve the Lord Christ with consequent abandonment of one's own life.

The shadow of the cross falls upon all those vital aspects of Christian experience which perplex true hearts. If only the cross were understood, many complaints would be silenced which murmur against God's providence. Many a counselling session in the pastor's study would be cut short by applying the meaning of the cross. It answers so many questions, not easily but profoundly.

If you have struggled to worship the Almighty, you will have learned that there is no satisfying communion with the Most High without a cross. Our Saviour arose a great while before it was day to draw near to his Father. Having no central heating, it is no stretch of the imagination to think that he shivered while his metabolism was still sluggish in early morning hours. Perhaps he felt the pain of prying his eyes open, for he was a true man who had spent long days and nights instructing the ignorant, convincing the gainsayers, and healing the sick. He did not have a good night of sleep before his secret hours of worship. Perhaps he had to stand lest he fall asleep. Perhaps these struggles led to his sympathy for his disciples in the Garden. When they slept instead of praying, he gently said, 'The spirit is willing but the flesh is weak'. Oh, he had felt the weakness of human flesh!

A cross greets the Christian who is determined to rise early to meet his God. It begins with the alarm clock. Self desires another hour of sleep. It is only reasonable to remain in bed since the baby woke up twice last night. But if the love of Christ burns in your soul, you would rather inflict pain on yourself than plunge into the demands of business at home and office, and end the day with the sad realization that you had not been with him in quiet at all.

Furthermore, to rise early in the day you must deny self of pleasant social evenings which tend to last into late hours.

And when you have managed to bring yourself to your devotions, stubborn self intrudes still. Thoughts of your affairs demand attention from your mind so that honest contemplation of the glory of God is crowded out. A thousand selfish interests prevent true prayer from ever beginning. Our Lord taught us that prayer begins when the heart cries 'Hallowed be thy Name'. It cannot be uttered until self-interest is ruthlessly yanked from the soul as a tooth is from your jaw. This is painful and pinching.

Preachers meet sad-eyed saints who would like them to recommend a good book on devotions, 'something to pick up my drooping spirits'. The place of private retirement has grown dull or unrewarding. Often behind the request is a desire to find a new secret to approaching God's courts, a little device or an easy step back to the place of joyful fellowship with God and the Lamb. There are no such books or devices. You must bear a cross! Take aim on self. Set your sights on putting self to death. Deny self! Fast! Rise earlier! Cry with a fresh uniting of all your energies for the one purpose of knowing the Lord. And tomorrow? The cross will be there again. And if you do not choose to inflict pain on self, you will relapse once more into coldness. You will withdraw to a distance from the Lord.

Some poor creatures have stopped seeking the joys of God's presence. Perhaps you have assumed that God will not show you his glory. On the contrary, he delights to make himself known. But there is a cross at the threshold of the secret place of the Most High. To come under the shadow of the Almighty you must put self to a slow, agonizing death.

The long shadow of the cross will follow you from your home to your field of service for the Lord. Faithful witnesses to Christ face dreadful pains. When you arrive at your shop, fellow workers may be gathered in a corner laughing and slapping shoulders. You know you dare not approach to join in. The subject of the good humour is filthy. During the day, as serious opinions are discussed, there is an opportunity to give the biblical view on issues of sin and righteousness or the purpose of life. But each time you speak, you have seen rejection of yourself with your views. Each testimony for truth makes you more unwelcome. Will you be bold for truth today?

Christians are sensitive. We want to be liked and accepted. It is pleasant to be agreeable and peaceful. It is our longing to become more intimate with fellow men. Some brutes witness with an attitude of 'I don't care what anyone thinks of me'. That is to be callous, not gracious. As God's grace quickens in us love for men, a sense of courtesy is heightened, a longing for gentleness and peace is increased. But with all of this our Lord's honour is at issue in the discussion. The eternal welfare of men's souls hangs in the balance with their understanding of truth.

What must the Christian do if he is to witness? He must consciously choose words that pain his own social consciousness and love of peace. He must purposely drive the wedge between self and fellow workers deeper! There are no easy steps to witnessing! No painless, unembarrassing methods! You must bring men to see that they are filthy sinners under the wrath of God who must flee to Christ for mercy. That is offensive. And there is no way to coat it with honey.

When a young woman explains the gospel to her mother, she may almost anticipate the cool reception. Whichever way the truth is presented, implied is the life-long error of mother. It is all a denial of her religion, her views, her life-style *from a daughter*. It cuts her heart like a knife. Yes, but when the sword of the Word cuts mother's heart, a sensitive daughter has at the same time chosen to drive spikes into her own flesh. Self has had to be crucified. Two hearts are broken, not merely one.

As the cross casts a shadow over worship and witnessing, its shades also fall upon all service to God. Questions like, 'Will you teach a Sunday School class?' become, 'Will you relinquish tranquil and amusing evenings which follow frenzied days in the office? Will you sacrifice relaxation seriously to study God's Word in preparation for the class? Will you spend scarce time to pray for your students?' Each duty assumed for the good of the Church imposes restrictions elsewhere.

An image of the cross is discernible everywhere in the Christian life. Our Lord was not speaking in hyperbole when he set before us a daily cross. To turn from it is to revert to the broad way which leads to destruction.

3

JOY BEYOND THE CROSS

'And he said unto them, Verily I say unto you, There is no man that hath left house, or parents, or brethren, or wife, or children, for the kingdom of God's sake, who shall not receive manifold more in this present time, and in the world to come life everlasting.' [Luke 18:29, 30]

Confronted with the unrelenting demands of the cross, some begin to think of Christianity as a grim and undesirable existence. When a truth lies ignored and forgotten, great emphasis must be given to it. But emphasis on 'daily' self-inflicted pain sounds austere if not gruesome. Gospel calls to take up one's cross may seem to be an invitation to take pleasure in self-abuse. It must then be made manifest that our wise Lord's demands cast no bitter pall over the Christian life.

Mention of self-denial is essential if we are to be faithful to any who are attracted to the benefits associated with trusting the Lord Jesus. Danger lurks for those who do not carefully count the costs of forsaking this present world to follow him. Enchanted with the bright prospects of the kingdom of God, some receive its announcement with joy. But 'when tribulation or persecution arises because of the word, by and by they are offended' [Matthew 13:21]. To avoid misrepresentation and to turn men from apostasy our Lord must clarify the reality of losing one's life to enter his kingdom.

Still, in our Lord's view, his own cross was not all

bleak. Hebrews 12:2 tells us that he *'for the joy* that was set before him endured the cross.' Even when his soul was troubled from taking full measure of the terrors of Golgotha, the only Saviour of sinners never lost sight of the joy beyond. Travail of soul would bring satisfaction. He would gather great spoil by his cross [Isaiah 53:11–12]. 'Wherefore [because he became obedient unto the death of the cross] God also hath highly exalted him, and given him a name which is above every name: that at the name of Jesus every knee should bow . . .' [Philippians 2:9, 10]. Just so, the only lasting and fully satisfying joys for any man lie on the other side of a cross.

Luke 18:18–30 preserves an outline of our compassionate Lord's interview with the rich young Ruler, and of a subsequent discussion occasioned by it. 'Come, take up the cross and follow me' were Jesus' final words to the seeker [Mark 10:21]. Abhorring the cross of denying self its beloved riches, the young man sadly abandoned the great Prophet. This inquirer would not inflict pain on himself in order to find eternal life. He desired heaven and all the pleasures of earth too. Then, it seems, the disciples sensed Christ's disappointment with the departure of the sinner.

As if to encourage our Lord, who himself was feeling the painful cross of spurned love, Peter spoke. 'We have left all, and followed thee.' Some men do not snub the cross, but will deny themselves, esteeming companionship with Christ a great boon at any price. Peter meant to console our noble Lord. But a selfless Jesus turned the occasion into an opportunity to comfort his disciples. Attention was given to the blessedness of those who suffer for the kingdom of God's sake.

Not one man has ever sacrificed for his Lord without being richly repaid. If the cross is only contrasted with earthly pleasures lost, it may seem hard and threatening. But when the cross is weighed in the balances with the glorious treasures to be had through it, even the cross seems sweet. As Samuel Rutherford wrote, 'Christ's cross is the sweetest burden that ever I bore; it is such a burden as wings are to a bird, or sails to a ship, to carry me forward to my harbour.' Or as the self-denying apostle wrote, 'For our light affliction, which is but for a moment, worketh for us a far more exceeding and eternal weight of glory' [2 Corinthians 4:17].

Perhaps the most astonishing part of our Lord's teaching to the disciples on this occasion was his reference to 'this present time'. Blessings for the cross-bearing servants of Christ are not all reserved for another world. Though their great inheritance is 'reserved in heaven' for them [1 Peter 1:4], God has granted his people a foretaste of heaven 'in this present time'.

A clear comparison is drawn, 'manifold more in this present time', 'more' than was left behind of houses, lands, parents, brothers, wife or children! The man who has denied self for Christ can never say he is a loser by it, even if the comparison is merely between benefits in this world as compared with losses. Careful auditing of each Christian's ledger arrives at confirmation of this balance: 'manifold more in this present time'. Though the pains of self-denial are nonetheless real, the fraternity of the cross is a bright and cheery society even now in life on earth.

Often our Lord grants manifold more in kind. More is given of the very object sacrificed. Peter had left all to follow Jesus. He had left a quiet fishing village for a tumultuous life of constant pressure by the crowds. He never again returned to the tranquil life of a fisherman. Yet he received a peace which the world cannot give [John 14:27]. Peace with a reconciled God, peace concerning the future, and peace flowing from the assured presence of the Son of God, filled his soul.

Peter was severed from a beloved father and other relatives. Many Christians have lost the affection of parents in confessing Christ. Some have been cut off from brothers, sisters and friends. Yet who are more deeply loved in the church than those who have paid the dearest price to declare their faith boldly. Saintly old men become fathers and older women mothers to the cross-bearer. What a vast number of brothers and sisters await him at the Lord's house! How many have found fellowship in the assembly of the redeemed more intimate and gratifying than a home lost for Christ's sake. We are replete with 'manifold more' in this present time.

Some Christians have found that a financial cross awaits them. It was this expectation which the 'Good Master' had set before the rich young ruler. His actual loss of gold would have been felt. But had he taken up the cross, thereby losing houses or lands, he would have received 'manifold more'. This is not a crass materialistic promise that our Lord will eventually multiply the bank account of any who follow him. But 'the earth is the Lord's and the fulness thereof' [Psalm 24:1]. And the God of all the earth has promised to add food, clothing and all other needs to those who seek first his kingdom [Matthew 6:33]. Rich men have seen their riches take wings and fly away. Some who once were wealthy are at this very moment destitute. But David could say, 'I have been young, and now am old; yet have I not seen the righteous forsaken, nor his seed begging bread' [Psalm 37:25].

Whatever your losses 'for the kingdom of God's sake' it will not take much imagination to discover 'manifold more' in kind given to you. With that in the background our Lord adds even greater bliss, 'and in the world to come life everlasting.' Ah! the world to come!

Ugly as the cross appeared in Gethsemane, do you think our Lord Jesus regrets his cross? While he sits upon the throne of God, around which many angels, the four living creatures, the twenty-four elders and thousands of spirits of men render perfect worship to him and sing 'Worthy is the Lamb', can there be any fretting over the cross?

Do you imagine that those who live in his glorious presence complain of crosses? When Stephen walks in his resurrected body in the heavenly Jerusalem where God himself shall dwell with him, how light an affliction will his stoning seem to be! If in this life Paul could say, 'For I reckon that the sufferings of this present time are not worthy to be compared with the glory which shall be revealed in us' [Romans 8:18], then a thunderous 'Amen' will brush aside crosses as nothing in glory.

Count it as a profound truth which Christ taught: 'Blessed are ye, when men shall revile you, and persecute you, and shall say all manner of evil against you falsely, for my sake. Rejoice, and be exceeding glad: for great is your reward in heaven: for so persecuted they the prophets which were before you' [Matthew 5:11,12]. Some become hypnotized by crosses. Their eyes are riveted on the cost of self-denial. Or they grumble that others have not such heavy crosses as they. Then comes the temptation to abandon the cross as the rich young Ruler did. Our Lord counsels, 'Rejoice and be exceeding glad' — think of your reward in heaven! You have joined the noble ranks of the prophets. Joy in his kingdom comes with a cross. Most of those who fail to experience the joy of the Lord have refused to take up a cross!

4

CHRISTIAN LIBERTY

For none of us liveth to himself, and no man dieth to himself. For whether we live, we live unto the Lord; and whether we die, we die unto the Lord: whether we live therefore, or die, we are the Lord's. [Romans 14:7, 8].

God's great truths are all inter-related. Each doctrine of God's Word touches every other. Thus is each axiom held in balance by all others. However, the human heart, through ignorance and laziness, tends to compartmentalize truths. It is common to find men isolating certain biblical information from all that surrounds it. When that is done, a doctrine begins to list as does a ship in danger and it threatens to sink into the deeps of error. We have all seen cults grasp a biblical teaching and distort it into untruth by removing the props of supporting doctrines.

Such danger arises frequently when Christians consider the biblical teaching of Christian liberty, particularly that aspect of liberty commonly called the *adiaphora*, or things indifferent. Believers are often tempted to forget that other truths stand close by Christian liberty to hold it erect as God intended. Recognizing a tendency to isolate this one doctrine, John Calvin began his discussion of the subject in his *Institutes* by saying, 'The moment any mention is made of Christian liberty lust begins to boil, or insane commotions arise, if a speedy restraint is not laid on those licentious spirits by whom the best things are perverted into the worst.'[1] History past and recent has shown that Calvin's concern was not unfounded.

There is a wonderful teaching in God's Word. In 1 Timothy 4:4 and 5 we are instructed that all of creation is good. No object formed by God's power is evil in itself. Everything in the world is to be received and used by man with thanksgiving. We are free to use all creatures for our comfort and for the praise of the Lord. Conscience need feel no hesitation in using the material world. Such a principle is grand and the source of much profit.

However, some have treated this teaching as if there were no other doctrines in the Bible to qualify and clarify it. Some who rightly appreciated that there must be self-denial at the very outset of the Christian life have put the biblical teaching of self-denial quite out of their minds when applying the truth that things are indifferent [neither good nor evil in themselves]. As a result many have plunged headlong back into self-indulgence. They begin again to serve themselves rather than the Lord.

In the name of liberty professing Christians glut themselves with luxuries, entertainments and sensuous pleasures. Under the banner of freedom men give the reins to their thirst for wealth, women dress immodestly, feeding vanity which loves attention, and youth abandon themselves to athletics and leisure. When self is fed in this manner it becomes brazen and runs to excess, crowding God out of the heart.

Behind many a Christian's fall into obvious

1. *Institutes* 3:19:1.

immorality has been the use of things indifferent to serve self. Liberty is turned to licence by self. Some have seen these abuses and have retreated from liberty to a new legalism. Both extremes are harmful. A biblical course must be sought.

There are two main passages in the New Testament in which Paul discusses the use of things indifferent: Romans 14:1–15:7 and 1 Corinthians 8–10. In both passages the apostle defends the Christian's liberty but he puts it on an even keel by mixing liberally his teaching on self-denial. Self-denial is of primary importance in comprehending Christian liberty without perversion. It keeps the ship of liberty from listing and carrying men to their ruin. Paul's appeal to self-denial is evident in the verses quoted at the head of this chapter.

Self-denial corrects two evil tendencies ever attacking Christian ethics. There is a tendency to give more attention to outward standards than to the inward state of the heart. And there is a tendency to be strict with others and lenient with oneself. Romans 14 will show you how these two dragons are slain by the sword of self-denial when their heads appear in the land of Christian liberty.

Paul finds at Rome two groups of believers in the same congregation. One group is vegetarian, the other eats meat. What are they to think of each other? The Spirit requires the one to judge the other with charity. You must look at those with contrary practices not as self-indulgent but as conscientiously acting with a desire to please the Lord. Verses 6–9 put great emphasis on this. You must give attention, not to the outward standard of conduct in the use of indifferent things, but to the inward motive. Your brother desires to glorify God in his practice. That should keep the meat-eaters from sneering at the vegetarians. And it should prevent vegetarians from censoriously judging meat-eaters and declaring them unspiritual.

Now you do not really know that such a conclusion is true of your brother; for you cannot look into his heart and read his motives. But both of you bow your heads before a meal and give thanks to God. Both are professing to eat unto the Lord. Therefore you are bound to assume that all his actions are for the glory of God. He is not serving self or lust but the Lord.

In our society there may be a Christian who cannot go to the beach without lusting after women dressed immodestly. So he denies himself the right to enjoy surf and sand. If he loves the ocean, it may be like plucking out a right eye of personal enjoyment in order to keep his conscience clear. But he is tempted to measure all men by his own experience. He is inclined to suspect that a brother goes to the beach in order to indulge lustful thoughts. He is tempted to legislate that no Christian is to go to a public beach. Paul is saying in effect, 'You have no right to pluck out your brother's right eye!' You are taught to deny yourself, but not to deny your brother. You must assume that his heart is pure, foreign as that may be to your experience. You must conclude, 'Just as I stay away from the beach out of devotion to Christ, he goes to the beach as unto the Lord, with a pure heart of thanksgiving to God. I am pleased that he can enjoy a part of God's creation that I cannot.'

But while you may in charity *assume* that a Christian brother acts from pure motives, you dare not *assume* that your own heart is upright. You must be more charitable to others than you are to yourself. You have no access to a fellow Christian's heart, no ability to test his inward devotion to the Lord, which is the all-important matter in using things indifferent. But you can scrutinize your own heart. You can examine your inner man to detect your own motives and aims for every act. Paul brings you back to this point. 'None of us liveth to himself.' All is 'unto the Lord.'

Christian liberty then does *not* teach that there are things in the world in which you are free to indulge yourself. It does *not* suggest that you may do anything you wish with God's creation. But it teaches that there are things which you are free to enjoy and use *as you serve the Lord*. And your eye is turned inward to discover whether your eating and drinking is unto him! A critical eye is turned away from your brother's practice; but it is turned to intense self-scrutiny. Examination is not focused on outward standards but upon inward motives.

In fact the exact opposite is often the method used even by Christians in determining conduct. Men turn their eyes away from self to others. An elder in the church goes fishing for relaxation. A young convert looks at him and concludes that if an elder fishes there can never be anything wrong with fishing. So he may fish to his heart's content with never a twinge of conscience. But he has looked away from self to another and has ignored the heart motives completely.

Furthermore he finds that another elder bowls. A deacon travels. A spiritual old saint collects antiques. All, all of these pursuits may be his too! Soon his life is so cluttered with the things which other Christians do that the Word of God is choked by the cares and riches of the world. Legitimate relaxation becomes an all-absorbing passion. God is served by none of his activities. Rather he has been nudged out of the soul. But was the young man not free to use his liberty? Unto the Lord, yes! In self-indulgence, no! 'None of us liveth unto himself.' 'We live unto the Lord.'

When this explanatory note is appended to Christian liberty, a careful watch over one's own soul will begin to eliminate 'things' which are not evil in themselves. To deny self and bring one's life into a course which will best glorify God, perfectly legitimate pleasures will be severed. The pleasure of indifferent things will be denied to self so that life may be lived unto the Lord. Others will be received still with praise and thanks to the Giver of every perfect gift. No two men will retain and cut off the same items. There is something childish and legalistic about churches in which all of the saints observe precisely the same standards. When all lives begin to sink into the same mould of denial and exercise of liberty, something is amiss.

In 1 Corinthians 9:1–6 Paul listed the legitimate things which he denied himself. He asserted his right to have them, but for the Lord's sake he pinched his flesh. A wife, a salary, certain food and wine were given up for the Lord's sake. Paul mentions this not to lead others to refuse marriage, wages and wine but to illustrate the necessity of self-denial. Can you, as Paul, list legitimate pleasures which you have denied yourself to honour the name of Christ? If you cannot be concrete perhaps you need again to ask whether your liberty is used to indulge the flesh or to serve the King, for those who fear living in scandalous adultery may feed the same flesh with a life of recreation. In 1 Peter 2:16 we are instructed to do well, 'as free, and not using your liberty for a cloak of maliciousness, but as the servants of God.' Liberty may be an instrument for giving glory to the Most High, or it may be a curtain used to shield base indulgence of the flesh. You may discover by self-examination of your heart which function liberty serves in your life.

Even further must the use of liberty be restricted. More is to be considered than the relative places of God and self in the soul. A pure motive to please the Lord in an exercise of liberty is not sufficient. Paul indicates that the well-being of other Christians must be desired above self-interest. He states it most forcefully in Romans 15:1–3: 'We then that are strong ought to bear the infirmities of the weak, and *not to please ourselves*. Let every one of us please his neighbour for his good to edification. For even *Christ pleased not himself.*' Self must be denied, but if one is going to imitate the Master, he must deny self for the brethren.

Christians who had consciences more tender than God's Word required are called 'the weak'. Because of personal opinions, not biblical instruction, they felt compelled to abstain from meat [v. 2] and wine [v. 21] and they felt obliged to observe certain religious days [v. 5]. Their consciences were more strict than the Word. They felt it would be a sin to eat meat, drink wine or fail to observe days. Other believers had a conscience no more demanding than God's Word on these matters. They were called 'the strong'. They felt no qualms about eating meat, drinking wine or abandoning the observance of days.

Paul is not suggesting that those who had well-instructed consciences in these matters were stronger servants of God in general. The designations 'strong' and 'weak' refer to particular matters of Christian ethics. It is quite conceivable that the same individual may be 'strong' as to eating meat but 'weak' as to the observance of days. And it is possible that the weak man is more spiritual in his entire life than is the strong. Only in particular matters is he over-scrupulous.

A man of 'strong' judgment may be very brutish of spirit. He may be insensitive to the fact that using his liberty in the presence of the weak may tempt his brother to follow his practice against a weak conscience. Thoughtless exercise of his liberty would then place a 'stumblingblock' or an 'occasion to fall' in the brother's way [v. 13]. The fall is not because eating meat is evil in itself, but because a man must not eat with a weak conscience [vv. 14, 23]. If he judges it to be sin and cannot eat in faith, to him it is sin. 'You must think about your brother's conscience, not merely your own', Paul is saying. Love for your brother will lead you to put him first [v. 15].

After denying yourself to glorify God, you must deny yourself to edify fellow Christians. 'Let us therefore follow after the things which make for peace, and things wherewith one may edify another' [14:19]. 'Let every one of us please his neighbour for his good to edification' [15:2]. Self must not be pleased first [15:1] and at the cost of pleasing a brother. That would not be edifying. How often the apostle qualifies Christian liberty with denial of self for the sake of other men. 'Brethren, ye have been called unto liberty; only use not liberty for an occasion to the flesh, but by love *serve one another*' [Galatians 5:13]. 'All things are lawful for me, but all things are not expedient: all things are lawful for me, but all things *edify not*' [1 Corinthians 10:23]. It is not enough to ask yourself, 'Does God's Word permit me to use these good things of the world? You must also inquire, 'Will it serve the glory of God?' and, 'Will it edify my fellow Christians?'

As John Brown has wisely written in his commentary on 1 Peter, 'No consideration should prevail on us for a moment to give up our liberty, but many a consideration should induce us to forego the practical assertion or display of our liberty.' When love for God and love for the brethren fill a Christian's breast and keep self under, there need be no fear of abusing the liberty of things indifferent. Such a man will never run to excess. Self will be denied and others pleased in the use of all things.

5

MARRIAGE AND SELF-DENIAL

Nevertheless let every one of you in particular so love his wife even as himself; and the wife see that she reverence her husband. [Ephesians 5:33]

Major New Testament passages on marriage make direct appeals to Genesis 1–3 for their notions and for their authority. A return to the creation account reminds us that God 'has determined . . . the bounds of our habitation' [Acts 17:26] in matrimony. By his moulding of human personality and his fashioning of the institution of marriage, the Potter has defined limits within which men and women may find marital satisfaction and happiness. 'Know ye that the Lord he is God: it is he that hath made us and not we ourselves; we are his people' [Psalm 100:3]. All creatures of clay who transgress the divinely set perimeter will come to conjugal grief.

Failures in marriage and shattered homes are multiplying in western society for three reasons, all of which relate to creation doctrine. First, spouses may be ignorant of the well-marked boundaries which God has set for them; or they may raise clenched fists of defiance against the Most High; or remaining corruption and slight progress in grace may prevent husband and wife from executing known precepts of the Lord. In any case, 'Woe unto him that striveth with his Maker' [Isaiah 45:9].

In the cradle of human history, Adam and Eve encountered realities of their very existence which were profoundly humbling. Having minds untainted by sin, our first parents read with comprehension the book of God's general revelation. No doubt as they walked with the Lord of hosts in the garden, they understood themselves quite well. From both members of the marriage union there was exacted selflessness by the very circumstances and composition of their beings. But in a sinless state humility and meekness were not laborious. No challenge of covetousness rose in their hearts to make self-denial painful. In a state of moral perfection, to live wholly unto others is unmixed joy.

The creation order published Jehovah's intended social order for men and women. Man inhabited the earth for a time before woman was brought into being. She was made from the man. Precedence of man to woman was not accidental. 1 Corinthians 11 and 1 Timothy 2 affirm a God-given directive intended in these circumstances. Man's pre-existence to woman and woman's derivation from man announce God's mandate for the *subordination of woman to man*. Man was made the social head of the woman.

Furthermore woman was created to fulfil the needs of man. 'The Lord God said, It is not good for the man to be alone. I will make *a helper* suitable *for him*' [Genesis 2:18 NIV]. Woman was informed of God's purpose in bringing her into this world. It was for the role of *helper*. It was *for him*. At the first wedding she took her name from man [2:23]. In wedlock she enters upon man's calling in a supporting posture. She had been made to assist and complement man. 1 Corinthians 11:9 emphasizes, 'Neither was the man created for the woman; but the woman for the man.'

The attempted reversal of these roles in our modern world is in defiance of the Creator. How readily provoked is the self-assertive spirit of fallen woman when the New Testment repeatedly calls her to submit to and reverence her husband (Ephesians 5:22, 24, 33; Colossians 3:18; 1 Peter 3:5]! But clearly the testimonies of Scripture are united. God expects women to yield to their husbands' lead and to serve his best interests. For a time Eve was free of any sense of self-importance and selfish ambition. She lived for the glory of God and for the good of her husband. Her contentment came in her supreme allegiance to her Maker and in doing his will as 'helper' for man.

The repetitions in Scripture of God's law that wives submit to husbands alerts us to the fact that a radical change in human affairs has come about. For a time there was a perfect marriage in the Garden of Eden. But a tragic fall of the human race came in a family context! God spoke to Adam [Genesis 2:15–17]. Man conveyed to woman what their Maker had forbidden in the Garden [cf. Genesis 3:2–3]. But Eve was isolated from Adam when new information was given her by the serpent. She thought that she could act independently. She knew more than Adam and need not consult him. Though his wishes were plainly expressed, she would make her own decision! Thus was Eve insubordinate to her husband on a matter of vital importance to their lives.

In consequence of this fatal mutiny from God's

arrangement and from her husband's authority, the Lord God said, 'Thy desire shall be subject to thy husband, and he shall rule over thee' [Genesis 3:16]. What had been the pleasure of her selfless existence before — submission to Adam's headship — has now an element of curse; for both she and her head are now selfish. Competing claims of self-interest will bring sorrow. Yet God's assigned order is unchanged.

Women continue to cringe before the divine mandate of submission to husbands. Desires to lead rather then follow recur. Temptations arise to take the dominant initiative in the family, to act as the head. But each instance of a wife failing to defer to the known wishes of her husband (unless those wishes oppose the moral law of God) subverts the divinely appointed order and multiplies misery in the earth.

Western society feeds the ego of women. With brazen directness it summons women to fight for their own rights. Educational systems, magazines, and advertising spawn self-assertiveness in her. Why should she not seek her own independent career? Why should husbands not be as much helpers to women as wives are to men? The psychological bombardment is having its self-seeking effects in modern woman to the ruin of homes.

However, woman was not the only spouse called to selfless service of another in marriage. When God had made Adam, even in an earth uncursed by sin, even in unspoiled fellowship with his Maker, man discovered a deficiency in himself. His gracious Lord recognized, 'It is not good for the man to be alone' [Genesis 2:18]. In a sense woman was the completion of man himself. She was the provision of what was lacking in him. He had a deep need for her.

When the Almighty escorted the first bride to Adam, unfallen man expressed the essence of marriage. 'This is now bone of my bones and flesh of my flesh' [Genesis 2:23]. In this pronouncement, our ancestor was not merely acknowledging Eve's literal origin from the rib taken out of his side. Adam did *not* say, 'She is what used to be bone of my bones.' Rather his proclamation was, 'This is *now* bone of my bones and flesh of my flesh.' As if to stress this matter, he adds, 'They shall be one flesh'! [Genesis 2:24]. In these observations, the first groom published God's *identification of the woman with the man.*

By marriage two lives are fused into one. Our Lord Jesus Christ confirmed the actuality of this union when he said, 'What therefore *God hath joined together*, let not man put asunder' [Matthew 19:6]. Paul recognized the identity of woman with man in marriage in Ephesians 5:28: 'So ought men to love their wives *as their own bodies.*' Taken alone this phrase is ambiguous. It could be understood to mean that men ought to love their wives in the same way that they love their own bodies. Rather Paul is riveting attention on the awesome reality of intimate conjugal union. His meaning is, 'So ought men to love their wives as (being) their own bodies.' Paul's next sentence confirms this intent. 'He that loveth his wife loveth himself.' As a matter of fact, your wife is your own body.

Implications of intimate marital union were far reaching for Adam. From the moment God brought the woman to Adam, he must think differently. He must no longer think of himself in detachment from his wife. She was his very body to nourish and cherish. Eve must be very central to all his considerations of time, employment, and thoughts. She must share in all as a wonderful part of himself. To be thoughtless of her would be as monstrous as neglect and abuse of his own body. She was henceforth a part of himself.

Many today love traditional wedding ceremonies with biblical language who would be repulsed if they comprehended the meaning. A pledge to take a woman for his wife commits a man to sharing life in its entirety. Man and wife are heirs together of God's gracious gift of one life [1 Peter 3:7]. It demands of him selfless thoughtfulness of her. We have observed fools who through sin have neglected and abused their bodies for intellectual pursuits. But it is apparent to all that a head which injures its own body is shameful. So is a man who fails to be considerate to his own wife in all her complex needs. Yet the New Testament repeatedly urges men to love their wives and be considerate towards them [Ephesians 5:25, 29; Colossians 3:19; 1 Peter 3:7]. Adam's early devotion to Eve was tragically altered.

When Adam and Eve had sinned, the holy Lord did not at first address both marriage partners. It was the head of the home whom he called to give an account. Adam's first family utterances as a fallen man are shocking. His attitude toward marriage had been profoundly reversed. Ignobly he answered God's searching inquiry about their sin with, 'The woman whom thou gavest to be with me, she gave me of the tree' [Genesis 3:12]! It would not be surprising if such a selfish remark incited a family brawl that night.

Adam's self-defence for his sin was a mental divorce of Eve. Cruelly he separated himself from his wife in his mind. Then he justified himself by shifting all blame to her. To rescue himself, he humiliated and endangered her. What had become of the lofty recognition that the two were one flesh? Was not Eve Adam's body now that sin had entered? Indeed she was just as much so as before! But Adam did not recognize it. It was base and selfish for him to banish her from the intimate union established by God. It was further rebellion against his Maker.

The fallen male mind is fully exposed in Adam's self-centred remark. Throughout the history of our fallen race men have abused women rather than nourished and cherished them. Selfish cruelty to wives has provoked self-defence in women and driven them to carnal responses in kind. Mental divorce of woman by the man is at the root of marital grief.

Desperate to have some time for himself, a husband retreats behind newspaper or television set or into bar rooms after his day's work. No communication is made from the head to his body (his wife). If she does not serve his interests, he becomes angry with her self-defence; but never does he take time to confer with her and to divulge his deepest concerns. Nor is an attentive heart directed to her signals of suffering or neglect. By his lead the two are no longer heirs of one life but strangers in a fractured existence. This tragic pattern, repeated to the misery of multitudes, begins with man's failure to recognize that his wife has been made by God a part of himself [Ephesians 5:33]. His private ego is too demanding to allow room for another as co-heir of his own intimate life.

Nowhere has selfishness done more damage than in homes. God's fundamental building-block for society is now displaced by self-assertion. Wives are too self-important to minister to their husbands. Their own names and careers are too significant for life to be wasted in helping husbands and living 'for them'. Husbands are too self-absorbed to share all of life with their wives, too self-centred to be thoughtful of and loving towards their spouses. Wisely the Scripture returns to the centre point. 'Wives, submit.' 'Husbands, love.'

Peace and joy will be encountered in any home where there is found a submissive wife and a solicitous husband. Even in the complex matter of sexual adjustment in marriage the Bible is not silent. A solution to all difficulties whatsoever in this aspect of life may be discovered in self-denial. 'The wife hath not power over her own body, but the husband: and likewise also the husband hath not power over his own body, but the wife' [1 Corinthians 7:4]. No explicit textbooks on physiology can touch the chief problem of sexual disharmony — selfishness. In any other marital strife, difficulties are resolved only by self-denial. Women must deny self to help and support husbands. Men must think first of the well-being of their beloved bodies, their wives.

Nothing is more distressing to pastors counselling a troubled man and wife than to hear from both competing claims of self-interest. Yet nothing is so common in marriage difficulties as to hear self-assertive remarks and to see self-devotion at grave cost to a spouse. How soon marriage counselling sessions would end if husbands and wives were competing in thoughtful self-denial. If the woman were anxious to yield to her God-given head in the home, and the man were ambitious to serve her comfort and welfare as being his own flesh, there would be no room for contention and strife. 'Wives, submit' and 'husbands, love' must be repeated until the message reaches beyond ears to the hearts of spouses.

Despite all the failure and sorrow in modern marriages, Christian young people should not hesitate to marry in the Lord. None are so well-equipped for the marriage state as children of God. The school of Christ is the finest training ground for living as husband and wife. In choosing a spouse, self-denial should be a characteristic sought after.

Who are better suited to wedlock than men and women who have already died to self? Already they live to serve and please Another rather than selfish desires. Even now they deny legitimate self-interests to wait upon One to whom solemn vows have been made. For him they daily take up a cross. In his school they have been taught to 'esteem other better than themselves' [Philippians 2:3]. In his service they have practised 'forbearing one another and forgiving one another' [Colossians 3:13]. In them is the fruit of the Spirit which includes 'longsuffering, gentleness, goodness, faith, and meekness' [Galatians 5:22, 23].

Those who live in the shadow of the cross are furnished with the self-denying graces required to build loving homes. If self-denial is practised in a household a generation of children will arise who have seen at first-hand what it is to love practically. Before their eyes will be parents whose love 'suffers long and is kind . . . envieth not . . . vaunteth not itself, is not puffed up . . . seeketh not her own, is not easily provoked . . . beareth all things . . . endureth all things.' What stronger commendation of the gospel could anyone give to children? What higher calling is in society than self-denial in marriage? It should have been so from the beginning. Now it may only be so by the grace of God which is found in Jesus Christ.

6

THE CHRISTIAN MINISTRY
AND SELF-DENIAL

For I have no man likeminded. who will naturally care for your state. For all seek their own. not the things which are Jesus Christ's. [Philippians 2:20,21].

'Self-centred Christian' is a term of impossible contradiction. A self-serving minister is one of the most loathsome sights in all the world. When the Great Shepherd calls a man to preach the gospel and shepherd his flocks, he issues a call to double denial of self.

An awesome dignity clings to the office of preaching the gospel. If a servant of Christ faithfully declares 'Thus saith the Lord', the authority of heaven attends his voice. 'It will be more tolerable for Sodom in the day of judgment than' for those who will neither receive nor hear the messenger of the Kingdom [Mark 6:11]. They are given an exalted privilege who are called to give their entire lives to the affairs of men's souls and to their eternal interests.

But our Master has not sent ministers into the pulpit with robes of state and a sceptre in hand. By his appointment pastors are to be girded with a towel, holding a basin for men's feet. Paul commended Timothy for displaying the true spirit of the ministry. 'He hath *served* with me in the gospel'. 'He has adopted the posture of a slave to others in the gospel work' is Paul's meaning.

In the Christian ministry *self-denial* must begin

with *an attitude regarding the calling*. Paul makes the heartbreaking observation that most fellow-labourers 'seek their own, not the things which are Jesus Christ's'. Timothy was an exception in his outlook on the ministry. We must admit in our hearts that Paul's observation is still true. This is the ugliest blemish in the modern clergy. Too many have lifted personal interests above the welfare of the sheep.

It can all begin so subtly. Christians applaud men with great public gifts in preaching and teaching. Excellent sermons feed the hungry and attract the lost. As a man's popularity rises everyone thinks it a pity that such marvellous gifts are being 'wasted' on a little congregation. This man's ministry is all-important. It is the great thing. An independent agency is set up to promote his ministry. Sheep are asked to support the project of speeding this man forward. Will they pray for him and give to him? He has this grand calling.

All is backward. He is called to pray for the sheep. His mission is to give to them. 'Ministry' means 'the serving of tables'. When a servant becomes self-important, what good is he? If he becomes enamoured with his servanthood and begins to speak of his great career as servant, he has misunderstood the meaning of the word! But in the ministry the servants are asking those who are to be served to step aside. They must not interfere in any way with the noble pursuit of servanthood. Modern churches give the distinct impression that the one who waits on tables is vastly more important than those who sit at tables. Certainly a church must value the gifts Christ has given her, but only for the service they render to the body.

Disciples of our Lord began to think of their callings as positions of honour to be grasped [Matthew 20:20–29]. Ambition seized the apostleship as an opportunity to climb a ladder of prestige. Then our Lord tersely said, 'Whosoever will be great among you, let him be your minister; and whosoever will be chief among you, let him be your servant.'

While others may 'seek their own things', a Timothean spirit 'seeks the things which are Jesus Christ's'. These things of Christ are precisely the well-being of his precious flock. Timothy 'will naturally care for your state'? Our glorious Lord, who richly deserved the servitude of every creature, did not grasp after position and reputation but 'took the form of a servant', we are told earlier in this chapter [Philippians 2:7]. He identified himself with the desperate plight of his people and came to serve their interests. 'The Son of Man came not to be ministered unto, but to minister, and to give his life a ransom for many' [Matthew 20:28]. 'His things' are supremely the well-being of the sheep for which he bled.

Our Good Shepherd has become the model for under-shepherds. His great concern is the good of the sheep. A good shepherd gives himself to the sheep. A thief comes to get something from the flock — wool or mutton. Jesus our Lord made every personal claim subservient to the blessing of his flock, even to giving his life that they might live.

Imitating the Great Shepherd, Timothy 'naturally cared for' the things concerning the saints. As a reflex he took their prosperity to heart. Paul used the same verb, *'care for'*, which our Lord used in the Sermon on the Mount: 'Therefore take no *anxious thought*, saying, What shall we eat? or, What shall we drink? or Wherewithal shall we be clothed?' Timothy was preoccupied with their spiritual state. He was concerned with their needs. Their state took precedence above his own things. It is for such ministers that the church looks today. Under this sort of man she thrives.

Attitudes toward one's calling into the ministry display themselves in a man's *bearing toward the flock* of God. Peter instructed, 'The elders which are among you I exhort . . . Feed the flock of God . . . Neither as being lords over God's heritage, but being ensamples to the flock' [1 Peter 5:1–3]. Arrogance and an overbearing spirit is never acceptable in elders. Popish demeanour reveals pride in the heart. Pompous and tyrannical treatment of subordinates almost universally attends positions of authority in the world and in human institutions. Never is such deportment permissible in elders. Our Chief Shepherd has said, 'Ye know that the princes of the Gentiles exercise dominion over them, and they that are great exercise authority upon them. But it shall not be so among you!' [Matthew 20:25, 26].

Christ and Peter are not addressing hypothetical possibilities, nor peculiar attitudes of ancient times. Self-importance and lording it over others is a shameful reality among modern ministers. Many young Christians have been seriously injured by the imperious ways of elders.

We live in an age when rebellion is common

against all divinely constituted authorities. Many have no respect for those whom the Holy Ghost has made their overseers [Acts 20:28]. Multitudes of local churches are ruined by anarchy. Christians must be taught to submit to Christ's order and to his assigned elders and deacons. Yet a church may be as much injured by tyranny as by anarchy.

At times there come challenges to issues of truth and righteousness which are vital to the glory of God and the well-being of the flock. Then pastors must know how to be insistent in their opposition to immorality and heresy. Their prophetic voices should thunder and their feet hold firm. But all issues are not so essential. Neither should a severe, authoritative stance be the characteristic feature of a pastor's bearing.

Some have imagined that with biblical commands to which the sheep submit, congregations could be coerced into non-resistance to the pastor's opinions and decisions. Zeal for truth and righteousness mixes with an inflated self-esteem in the elders. Other men are not led by example but suppressed by the worst of worldly tactics. Disagreement and questioning are rigorously stamped out. When elders become obsessed with the submission of the flock, they have a view dangerously close to the autocracy of Rome. That outlook involves an egotism from which ministers must be delivered.

Some elders never appreciate the compliment given them when a saint disagrees with the pastor's exposition of a text. At least the Christian under his care is devoted more to Scripture than to the man in the pulpit. Under his ministry the child of God has reached a maturity to think through issues for himself and has imbibed a Berean spirit [Acts 17:11]. But some ministers cannot endure the process of maturing in the sheep. At times parents are so flattered by the dependence of children that they cannot bear to see them grow independent with passing years. A swollen image of self-importance suffers too much for them to relinquish the reins. It is even so with domineering ministers.

Self-inflated leaders of God's flock poke their noses into a Christian's personal business beyond all reasonable bounds of decency and prudence. Pastors by counselling and visitation at times give directives and advice in matters that should not concern them. Under these sanctified busybodies the sheep are in bondage. Every aspect of life is under microscopic scrutiny and liable to demands made by an over-zealous pastor. Children must run to him for decisions which are to be made in all matters. It is with a sigh of relief that some sheep escape such ministries.

Other sheep have fixed character traits which are evident to everyone in the body. Awkward habits and tendencies make a certain brother less useful in the church than he might be. His sin-related quirk of personality is a bit troublesome to the assembly. Frustrated that gentle rebukes and patient entreaties have not cleansed the blemish from Christ's sheep, some elders take the rod of church discipline in hand to beat out the spots. In this is an abuse of church discipline which God intended to be used for extraordinary and public sins. Involved too is an audacity which decides that advancement in sanctification must be made at once! But no elder has been called to chart the timetable of growth in grace. It is not the place of elders to demand. Sheep cannot be whipped and driven into conformity with pastoral wishes.

Lording it over the flock provokes church fights and splits. A domineering spirit in elders provokes mature men of strong minds and independent judgment to leave the church. These very ones would have the greatest potential for future leadership in the assembly. Dictatorial measures make lesser men craven and dependent, stunting their true growth. But it also has its harmful effects on the 'lords over God's heritage'. It makes them egotistical and self-serving.

Predominant in an elder's bearing toward the sheep must be patience and meekness in his service. An exemplary walk must be his. Elders should be ensamples even in lowliness of mind and kindness. This ought to be demonstrated in showing deference to other elders in their opinions and rule. A pastor should show his flock how to be subject to other officers. He must not be too much in love with his own views to endure a barrage of disagreement.

Ministers must know how to lose arguments on non-essential matters. Care must be taken not to harangue others into silence. Preachers have a way with words. Their whole career is related to the skilful communication of ideas. It is a disgraceful fact that some ministers love to talk and have a habit of dominating discussion on every subject. Even when ignorant on an issue, a preacher can usually out-talk knowledgeable men. Thus in a controversy it is possible to silence men by sheer force of verbiage without convincing them. How exemplary would it be if all ministers exercised self-control over their tongues in the church! It is to be feared that some men are able to handle texts of Scripture who cannot discipline themselves.

With all of these abuses bringing the Christian ministry into disrepute, self-denial is sorely needed among pastors. There is no room for ostentation and lordly tactics. Imitation of Jesus Christ is needed. He was feared by the Pharisees whose mouths he stopped. But he was meek and lowly of heart to sinners, approachable by outcasts and children. Selflessness was displayed in his bearing. May God make it a leading feature in his ministers' comportment!

In the ministry *self-denial* is usually demanded *in the realm of material possessions*. It should come as a surprise to no one that few ministers become wealthy. Yet idealistic minds often fail to observe the obvious. Young men choose a calling with thoughts only of their preference for one sort of labour. They do not think of economic implications; they do not count the cost. Only after entering the work do they realize that for a lifetime they are locked into certain financial limitations.

You need only overhear ministers at clerical gatherings to realize that some have never counted the cost. Two curses of ministerial conferences are a spirit of levity and the discussion of salaries. It is gratifying that Reformed conferences are more free of these than most. Preoccupation with one's estate and financial security is a double abomination when found in clergymen. Ministers must have a spirit of sacrifice regarding riches.

A few would think it unfitting to mention finances in connection with the ministry. But these are more scrupulous than the Bible, which never hesitates to verbalize the concerns of men's hearts. An elder must not be 'greedy of filthy lucre' [1 Timothy 3:3]. Those who oversee the flock must not be motivated by a desire to get gain [1 Peter 5:2]. Especially those who 'live of the gospel' [1 Corinthians 9:14] must lay aside modern dreams of affluence and luxury.

Paul could say, 'I have coveted no man's silver or gold' [Acts 20:23]. Again, he said, 'I seek not yours but you' [2 Corinthians 12:14]. After giving to the poor and serving all, 'the Son of man had not where to lay his head' [Luke 9:58]. Are you in this school of self-denial? By God's grace, our day has seen numerous men who have financially sacrificed to a high degree and with never a word of complaint. They have been true lovers of the doctrines of grace and lovers of small flocks of true believers. Even so, Reformed circles are not completely free of grasping ministers.

Sometimes our offended Lord has found it necessary to rebuke a mercenary spirit in his servants. 'Who is there even among you that would shut the doors for nothing? neither do ye kindle fire on mine altar for nothing' [Malachi 1:10]. At the silvermine which lures Christians from the road to the Celestial City, John Bunyan wisely stationed a covetous preacher. It is Demas who loved so dearly this present world. 'If the parson may fiddle, mayn't the people dance' with earthly riches?

Though 'the labourer is worthy of his hire' [Luke 10:7] and he that sows to men spiritual things ought to reap their carnal things [1 Corinthians 9:11], carnal things must be rooted out of preachers' hearts by practised self-denial. Ministers' expectations must ever be directed to 'a crown of glory that fadeth not away' [1 Peter 5:4]. This true reward will be extended in the hand of the Chief Shepherd when he shall appear. If wages and bank accounts preoccupy your mind more than momentarily, perhaps it is time to hang up your preaching shoes. Jacob served seven years for Rachel, and the love of his heart made waiting for his reward seem 'but a few days'; so must love for Christ and his people captivate the hearts of ministers.

No more practical instrument will attend ministers in cultivating the gardens of the Lord than self-denial. No grace is more Christ-like. No cloak is so becoming to servants in his house.

PRAYER

'And Asa cried unto the Lord his God, and said, Lord, it is nothing with thee to help, whether with many, or with them that have no power: help us, O Lord our God; for we rest on thee, and in thy name we go against this multitude. O Lord, thou art our God; let not man prevail against thee.' [2 Chronicles 14:11]

Asa, king of Judah, one day stood in a place where every minister of the gospel has been. As God's people faced vicious enemies, he was their leader. It cannot be said that every instant in the pastorate is filled with fierce conflict; but the moments of respite are more surprising than the battle. The Great Shepherd has sent his sheep to live among wolves. This glorious Sovereign conducts the affairs of his everlasting kingdom 'in the midst of his enemies'. He builds his church in the neighbourhood of the gates of hell, recruiting each new member of his body from Satan's precinct. It is then inevitable that every preacher contends for truth and righteousness against principalities and powers of darkness.

Assaults are made upon our congregations just as Zerah the Ethiopian attacked Judah. Humanism, materialism, and hedonism have enlisted overwhelming forces to march against a few believers. The church on earth is in a state of war. She is ever engaged in combat.

Asa heard of Zerah's invasion, and advanced to meet the enemy. Leading about 600,000 troops the king seized the offensive. Marching against him were a million soldiers who had with them 300 chariots (the swift and feared machines of death in the arsenals of those times). Asa whipped the invaders soundly; for God came down and fought for Judah. God was greatly glorified. The Ethiopians were 'broken before the Lord,' and 'the fear of the Lord came upon' all nearby cities. The opposing forces were not merely stunned but demolished beyond recovery. There would be no regrouping for another charge.

What pastor would not love to see the forces of unbelief and sin put to flight in our day? It is the desire of every true man of God to deliver decisive blows against the batteries of hell. Our desire is that the Names of our Lord and our Father might be exalted upon earth in fresh victories. Oh, for multitudes to be awed into an awareness that the Most High dwells still in the midst of his people! If only the Almighty would bare his right arm in crushing his and our enemies, making the whole world of evil stagger before his Word!

Ezra, the writer of Chronicles, describes for us the determining factor of the ancient war. His account should captivate every heart in which there burns a holy zeal for the Lord of hosts. There was an enormous clash of arms at Mareshah, but nothing is recorded of the Israelites' skill in handling sword or bow. No doubt Asa and his captains carefully drew up their battle plan. Perhaps an ambush was set for the Ethiopians. Perhaps Zerah was outflanked. But Ezra is silent as to the strategy employed; for it was not the decisive element in the struggle.

The passing over of these aspects of the combat may disappoint some pastors. Ezra frustrates those who have become convinced that all hope of victory lies in our skill in handling our offensive weapons. Their entire attention has been turned toward the academic sharpening of men's swords and to the mastering of precise homiletical skills. Ezra completely exasperates the new cult of methodology. 'How to' experts with new programmes and schemes will read Chronicles in vain for tactics. Such silence instructs us that useful ministers must demolish the golden calf of activism.

'I will. tell you where the battle was won, where the critical manoeuvre was performed,' says the servant of God who records the smashing victory. So we follow the old priest backward in time to a moment before the actual bloody encounter. The first archer has not yet drawn his bow! But we are moving behind the front lines where historians wait with notepads to record statistics and tactics. We are led to a tent where Ezra lifts the flap. Within is a man, a solitary man, on his face in prayer!

There you have the secret weapon of Judah. When Paul was reviewing the Christian's armour in Ephesians 6, he admired this instrument of spiritual warfare and named it 'all-prayer'. It discharges the most lethal force ever known, rendering atomic weapons insignificant by its side. Every time great exploits have been done by the people of God, this fieldpiece has been rolled out by men of like passions with themselves.

A complete history of this mighty implement of warfare would recall the names of Moses, Elijah, Asa and Daniel. Topping the roll of honour in its skilful use is our holy Lord Jesus Christ. Since his day, it has been manned by the apostles, Luther, Tyndale, Knox, and Edwards. But the list is enormous. By it many an obscure pastor has secured triumphs of great importance to the kingdom of God. Their hours alone with God are yet untold. Even where known men of prayer have brought this secret force into service, their souls' exercises have been too sacred to be revealed in full. Will these holy seasons be recounted in the everlasting kingdom?

When we review the glorious annals of 'all-prayer', our faces begin to colour with shame! Alongside the great warriors who mastered this weapon we are mere dwarfs. Why are not the forces of unbelief and brazen sin driven back in our generation? Our hearts know that, at least in part, the answer is, 'We have not because we ask not' [James 4:2]. Our Lord has not retired 'all-prayer' to a museum where it becomes a curious relic of past exploits. It has been given into our hands! Yet we are unskilled in its use.

In 1651 ministers of the Church of Scotland drew up a humbling acknowledgement of the sins of the ministry. It was a confession to their God. One section of self-condemnation reads, 'Seldom in secret prayer with God, except to fit for public performance; and even then much neglected, or gone about very superficially.' In other portions the confession exposes the roots of prayerlessness: 'Finding of our own pleasure, when the Lord calls for our humiliation', and 'covetousness, worldly-mindedness, and an inordinate desire after the things of this life, upon which followeth a neglect of the duties of our calling, and our being taken up for the most part with the things of this world.'

Today, as then, it is easy to bemoan the theological confusion and the immorality of the age, but it is difficult to be humbled to prayer. Victories are not won by our hands, and enemies are not vanquished, because we do not pray. Isaiah's complaint is appropriate to our times, 'There is none that calleth upon thy name, that stirreth up himself to take hold of thee' [Isaiah 64:7].

But the painful acknowledgement that we do not pray is not sufficient. A further question must be asked. Why do we not use this great weapon which would prove devastating to our enemies?

One prominent answer must be that we cringe from the biting self-denial required in prevailing prayer. There is a definite cost to ourselves which makes us shrink back with horror from wrestlings in the place of private prayer. When we contemplate laborious prayer, all flesh which remains in us cries out with cowardly pleas for pity. Certainly our souls remember with fondness the privilege of drawing near to God in prayer, the joy of communing with the Holy One. But our flesh recalls the toil of prayer which pinches. Asa's laying hold of God demonstrates the self-denial required by exertion in prayer.

Self-denial is demanded in the circumstances of prayer. Note when it was that Asa 'cried unto the Lord his God'. It was at the moment when he commanded an army of 600,000 men. He was ruler of an invaded nation. Vital decisions were to be reached as he set the battle in array. Scouting reports must be examined. Counsels of war must be convened with the chiefs of staff. So many concerns lay claim to his time. None could be ignored nor sacrificed. Yet there was an inward compulsion to pray. He simply could not neglect urgent business. He must set his own ease aside. While others eat, sleep, relax or bolster their courage, Asa will pray.

Self must be denied as to *time* and attention for prayer. All-prayer cannot be wielded without the expenditure of time. 'A minute with God' seldom lays hold of him. Sustained prayer is necessary. Such time may only be found by snatching it from personal pursuits, however legitimate they may be.

Ministers of the gospel find their schedules squeezed. Families may not be forsaken in order to give time for prayer, for a well-regulated home is a prerequisite to the holding of the office of elder. God's flock may not be abandoned. There are lost sheep to be sought, straying sheep to be warned, lambs to be instructed. For all these souls an account must be given. Time for study may not be surrendered. If a man is to feed the flock of God, meditation, reading, diligent search of the Word is indispensable. When then will a minister find time to pray? Tomorrow will offer no more leisure. The time can only be located in what the minister might call 'his own time'.

It is striking that the greatest men of prayer in history have been some of the busiest men in the world. Think of Moses forging a nation from more than two million slaves. Or look at Daniel occupied with affairs of state in Babylon. Think of Luther — professor, Bible translator, pastor, prolific writer — who prayed three hours each day. But the chief example of them all is our Lord Jesus Christ who reserved early morning or late night hours for prayer. If anyone was entitled to relax, or seek refreshment, it was our holy Master. But he used his own time to pray. It is not that we are too busy to pray but that the flesh is still too insistent on satisfaction.

Days of fasting and prayer will be set aside from only one part of the calendar — yours! Days of relaxation and recreation must be shortened. Holidays must diminish. Self must be intentionally denied that you might come to your knees. How is it that ministers are too busy to be found in God's courts, but somehow the holidays are fitted in?

Self must be denied as to *energy* for prayer. There is something desperately arduous about protracted prayer. Even when it is full of delight and blessed nearness to our beloved Lord, it leaves a man drained of strength. David Brainerd jotted notes about prayer in his diary, such as 'extremely weak and overcome'. Martin Luther said, 'It is a tremendously hard thing to pray aright.'

King Asa must have expended much energy simply to the task of giving wholehearted attention to the throne of grace. He was facing his first day ever on a battlefield. Who can blame him for distracting fears and imaginings? Should he conserve his strength for the combat? But the kind of prayer recorded is made by virtue going out of the petitioner. As Moses prayed at the battle with Amalek in Rephidim, his hands grew tremulous long before the battle was won. When Jacob wrestled with God, he limped away from Peniel. If you have never felt your soul poured out before the Lord with a consequent exhaustion, it is doubtful whether you have advanced far in the school of prayer.

Recalling strenuous effort in the secret place, a pastor's flesh begins to make many a falsely pious suggestion when the hour of prayer approaches: fascinate the mind with another chapter of theology; rush off to visit a weak Christian; look through periodicals – to keep abreast of the times, of course – visit a loved bookshop! Anything is easier than an earnest conference with the living God. It will sap energy from self to lay hold upon the Lord until he visit your corner of the vineyard with grace and power.

Beyond the circumstances, stern self-denial is demanded as prayer is exercised. If a cross is felt at the doorway to the secret place of prayer, it is even more keenly experienced before the throne of grace. Many hours of wrestling in secret are times of combat with self. Even on our knees, even in the presence of the all-glorious King, self asserts itself frightfully.

No doubt Ezra has only given us a glimpse of the supplications of Asa. These come from the moment in which he *really* prayed and prevailed with God. Before the utterance of 2 Chronicles 14:11 fell from his lips, it is probable that effort after effort had been sent heavenward. Requests were composed and sent aloft only to fall back upon his own head. Certain heart attitudes of the king had to be refined before he could pray with such efficacy.

At the moment of prayer the renunciation of self-confidence is essential. Asa described his army as 'them that have no power'. How often may his pleas have been offered with delight in the remarkable strategy he and his captains had already set in motion? Little more would be done than implore God to bless the preparations for battle, which he already hoped would succeed. How long was it before Asa believed and felt in his heart that there was no help in man?

Then perhaps a struggle with despair would ensue. Discerning that he and his army had 'no power', what was the sense in praying? Once self has been stripped of all confidence, it will attempt to retain a position of importance by arguing that if there is no help in self, there is no help at all! What a struggle it is to believe at one and the same instant that with man, including self, there is no power, yet it is nothing for the Lord to accomplish our desires! 'Lord, it is nothing with thee to help . . . with them that have no power.' An effortless word from the Almighty executes all his pleasure in the affairs of this earth.

How common it is for pastors to kneel with a smile in the soul, a smile satisfied with preparations already completed for the pulpit. The illustrations are so plain; doctrinal formulations must be convincing; organization is thorough. Never should less be offered if it is in our power to master a text. But while self-confidence remains, the heavens are brass. Prayers do not penetrate. Only when confidence in self is mortified can we pray.

When self-impotence is felt by the preacher, the most desperate step has yet to be taken. He must assault the last bastion of self, that sulking unbelief in which self insists that if it cannot have the glory, no one will. Only when that hill is stormed, when self is slain, when the infinite majesty and power of the Lord appears to the eye of faith, only then does right earnest prayer begin. Without him we can do nothing. Yet nothing is too hard for our God. What mighty men of prayer we would be if these truths always gripped our hearts!

At the moment of prayer the renunciation of self-interest is essential. Asa's entire concern in the recorded entreaty is the glory of God. A sledge-hammer cry from his lips rocked the very foundation of heaven. 'Let not mortal man prevail against thee!' Again, how many sincere and spirited requests may have reached God's throne in earlier hours? 'O Lord, I am no experienced warrior; preserve my life!' 'O Lord, pity my family; don't leave my children fatherless!' 'O Lord of hosts, deliver me from utter failure in my first combat!' But as time wore on, Asa's self-interest melted as the dew in the heat of true prayer. His soul was absorbed in the glory of the God of Israel.

'Hallowed be thy Name' is the first petition of genuine prayer. Anyone can mouth the words; but it is no easy matter to make the request with heartfelt desire. Once the Son of God sweat blood before he could say, 'Not as I will, but as thou wilt' [Matthew 26:39]. Yet this grip alone will lay hold of God. Rightly implicating God's glory and honour in the object we seek moves the throne of God. It must not be done mechanically, but with a sincere craving for God to be praised.

Do you commonly pray until your fame, fortune, life and success pale into insignificance? until your soul is consumed with a sense that your Lord's honour is all-important? until you honestly seek only the public display of his glorious majesty? At such times pastors no longer seek something to say before the people or success in their ministries. Usually a fearful inward battle precedes such praying; for selfishness is very deeply rooted even in preachers' hearts. They too can 'ask amiss'. Indeed prayers for church and pulpit can arise from impure appetites [James 4:3].

The consequences of the king's believing and disinterested prayer were publicly known and were recorded for all generations to observe. God attended Asa on the battlefield. The Invincible Warrior went with him because there was more to Asa than his public efforts in combat. Had the leader of Judah's armies been only a public figure, giving himself to frantic, visible activity, another conclusion would have been written to these historic events. But Asa retired, denied himself, prayed. 'Thy Father which seeth in secret shall reward thee openly' [Matthew 6:6]. Only God's eyes penetrated the doors of Asa's tent, but all the world observed God's answer to his prayer. Open blessings in response to secret devotional exercises are a promise from him who cannot lie.

One of the sorriest creatures in all the world is a preacher who does not pray, except in public. Even with the theology of Calvin, the illustrations of Spurgeon, and the searching applications of Edwards, if a pastor has not been alone with God in secret, he is a pitiful figure in the pulpit. Without secret prayer he is without unction, a lifeless shell. Though ministers may, as other true saints, fall into intervals of prayerlessness, he is no man of God in whom this condition prevails. He is a hypocrite who is all superstructure in plain view with no unseen foundation. Bright flowers without roots are plastic, having no life.

Spiritually discerning men detect periods in our ministry when the sharp edge has been removed from pulpit efforts. Something is not quite the same as it has been. They would be hard pressed to express why it is so. It is the same man preaching, using the same gifts, including the same external elements of a sermon. But the Lord does not send the Word as a shaft into the hearers' hearts. Often the cause is neglect of this strange weapon. It is an instrument never carried into the battlefield, but used in secret — all-prayer!

When decline in pulpit effectiveness is noted, it is time to return with sorrow to that confession by Scottish ministers in 1651: 'Exceeding great selfishness in all that we do; acting from ourselves, for ourselves, and to ourselves. Seldom in secret prayer.'

Young men entering the ministry have visions of great exploits for the Lord. They should know that men who have been twenty or thirty years in the service of God and his people once had visions too. True men are stirred with hopes of shaking the world system with 'Thus saith the Lord', hopes of bringing the entire populace of a region under the fear of God, hopes of making the name of Jesus so desirable that he is generally sought after. There is a great gulf between such hopes and reality. Why we have not been the instruments of God's working that we had hoped to be requires no clever analysis — too much public activity with too little secret prayer; failure to master the use of all-prayer.

If a man sets out to excel this generation of ministers, he will find it easier to preach than to pray. In the stern reality of the secret place a dagger is placed in his hands. Timid men shrink back from using it. When a man will plunge the knife into self-pleasing, self-confidence, and self-interest, and will wrestle alone with God for his glory, the world will see God working openly, and granting victory on the field of battle.